Scott's boat reached the Antarctic in January 1911. It had to get there in the Antarctic summer, so the ship could break through the ice to get to land. After setting up camp, the men had to wait through the long, dark Antarctic winter. Only in the following summer would it be warm and light enough to set out for the South Pole.

Scott's boat, the *Terra Nova*

Base camp

Scott and his team set up a base camp. They had brought a wooden hut with them, cut into sections, which they put together. The walls were packed with seaweed to keep out the wind and cold. Even in the Antarctic summer, the temperature is only two degrees **Celsius** – just above freezing.

base camp

While they were waiting for the Antarctic summer, Scott and his team studied penguins.

woollen and windproof clothes

strong leather boots

Scott inside the base camp hut

5

Setting out

During the long Antarctic winter, when the temperature had dropped to minus 40 degrees Celsius, Scott sent out a group of four men with two motor sledges to drop food and **fuel** along their **route**.

one of the motor-powered sledges that Scott's team used

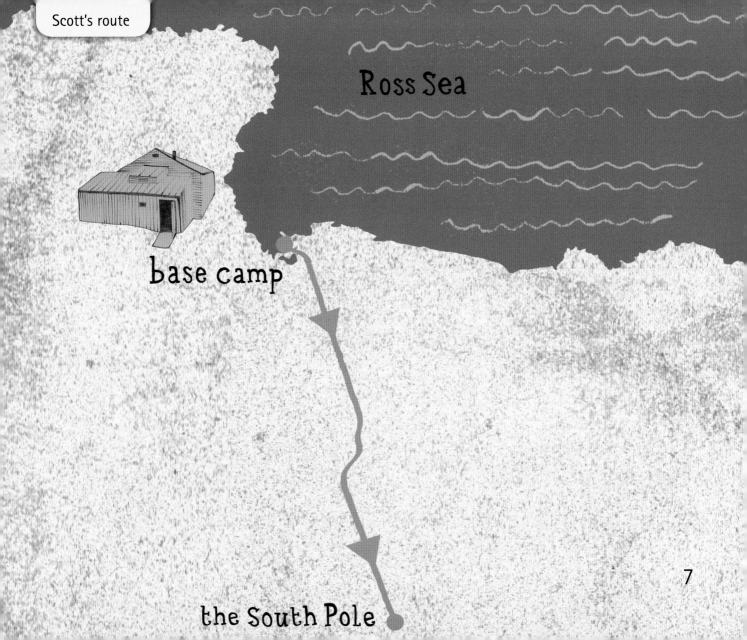

Ross Sea

base camp

the South Pole

7

On 2 November, 1911, Scott and nine other men set out with ponies. The final four men followed later with dogs. The South Pole was nearly 1,500 kilometres away.

8

Ponies and dogs were used to pull the sledges.

9

The motor sledges broke down after 80 kilometres. The ponies were not used to the freezing weather and, one by one, they died. The dogs were sent back to base camp because there was no food left to feed them. Now the men had to pull the sledges themselves. The men needed extra food, but Scott had not made any plans for this. They grew weaker and began to slow down.

The men used skis on the soft snow.

11

The South Pole

Scott planned that most of the men would turn back at stages along the way. Only five men made the last step of the journey to the South Pole. Scott reached the South Pole on 17 January, 1912, 76 days after they had set out.

This is the last photograph of the five men together, taken at the South Pole.

But they were not the first to get there.
Another explorer, **Norwegian** Roald
Amundsen had beaten them.
Bitterly disappointed and very tired,
the men were faced with the same
journey they had just completed to get
back to base.

Amundsen's tent, flying the Norwegian flag at the South Pole

Food

Scott and his men ate frozen seal meat, dry biscuits, raisins and a mix of fat and dried meat called pemmican. They boiled water for making tea or cocoa to warm themselves up. If the weather was good, the men walked for over nine hours each day. But pulling the sledges for about 19 kilometres a day was very tiring work.

the food store at base camp

the dried pemmican Scott and his men had

Illness

The weather got worse, with strong, freezing winds. The men got **frostbite** in their fingers and toes, which made them turn black and go numb. The bright sunshine and the white snow hurt the men's eyes and they got **snow blindness**.

They were losing weight and their food rations were too small. One of the men died in his sleep. Another man knew he would not make it back, so he walked out of the tent and was never seen again.

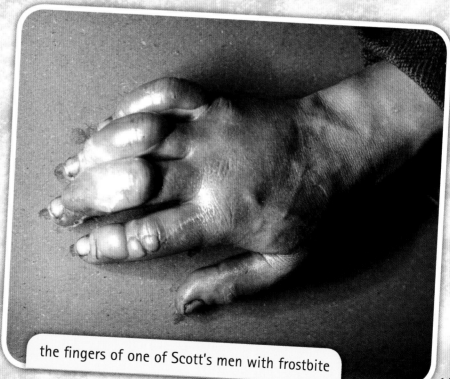

the fingers of one of Scott's men with frostbite

Blizzard!

Soon they became too tired to walk more than about nine kilometres each day. By the time the remaining three men made their final camp, their food had run out. Scott decided to stay with the sledges and send the other two men to get supplies from the food camp 18 kilometres away. They would get there faster without pulling sledges.

A terrible **blizzard** came. The two men set off, but they couldn't see where they were going and they were forced to turn back. They waited inside the tent for the storm to end.

The end

The temperature dropped to minus 40 degrees Celsius. Scott had been keeping a diary, and on 29 March, 1912 he wrote: "The end cannot be far. It seems a pity but I do not think I can write more." Without food, or fuel to heat water, they could not survive.

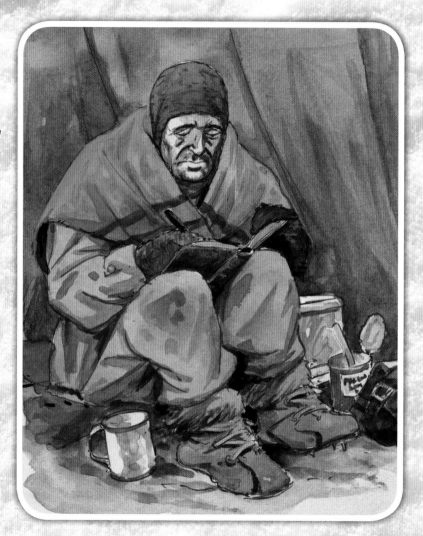

Eight months later, on 12 November, 1912, their tent was found, along with the bodies of the three men. A **monument** was made with blocks of ice and two skis.

Captain Scott – hero?

Many people think that Scott's journey was badly planned. Without dogs, the men had to do too much work. They didn't take enough food to make up for the hard work of pulling the sledges, or for delays because of bad weather. But Scott was a brave explorer and one of the first men to reach the South Pole, so to many people he is a British hero.

Glossary

blizzard	a snow storm
Celsius	a scale of temperature where water freezes at zero degrees and boils at 100 degrees
fuel	material to burn for heat, like oil
frostbite	injury to the body, especially the nose, fingers and toes, caused by freezing weather
monument	something placed over a grave to remember the dead
Norwegian	a person from Norway
route	the way of getting from one place to another
snow blindness	temporary blindness caused by brightness of the sun on the snow

Scott's journey through Antarctica

base camp

Scott's journey to the South Pole

Scott's journey back to base camp

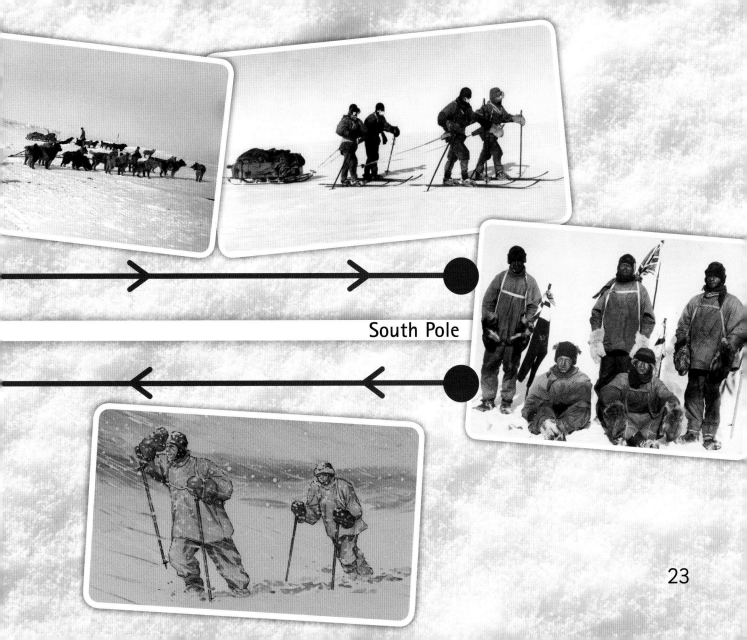

South Pole

23

Ideas for reading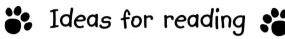

Written by Clare Dowdall, PhD
Lecturer and Primary Literacy Consultant

Learning objectives: read independently and with increasing fluency longer and less familiar texts; know how to tackle unfamiliar words that are not completely decodable; draw together ideas and information from across a whole text; give some reasons why things happen; explain organizational features of texts including alphabetical order, layout, diagrams, captions, and bullet points; explain ideas and processes using imaginative and adventurous vocabulary and non-verbal gestures to support communication

Curriculum links: Geography; Citizenship: Choices

High frequency words: is, on, the, at

Interest words: blizzard, Celsius, fuel, frostbite, monument, Norwegian, route, snow blindness

Word count: 744

Resources: globe, whiteboard, internet, books on Captain Scott

Getting started

- Tell children about a time you have felt cold. Describe what it felt like and ask children to share their experiences, writing a list of adjectives on the whiteboard to describe being cold.

- Read the title together. Explain that this is an information book about a journey to the South Pole and describes a true event. Read the blurb together. Discuss what children know about the South and North Poles and find them on a globe. Challenge children to predict what happened when Captain Scott went to the South Pole.

- Look at the photographs provided on the cover. As a group, list the information that can be retrieved and deduced from these illustrations, e.g. he travelled by sledge; he wore fur to keep him warm.

- Turn to the contents list and read it together. Discuss how the information in the book is organized and whether children think they need to read it in order or can dip in and out of chosen sections.

Reading and responding

- Turn to pp2–3. Introduce the word *Antarctica* and help children to read it by finding smaller words within it, e.g. *Ant-arc-tic-a.*